The Number Three

Barbara Taragan
Illustrated by Debbie Pinkney

Goldilocks sees three flowers.

Goldilocks sees three chairs.

Goldilocks sees three bowls.

Goldilocks sees three beds.

The three bears come home.

The three bears see Goldilocks.

The three bears wave goodbye!